Love the Babies

author/artist: Kathlyn Glover
design: Robert Lombardo

visit: LoveTheBabies.com

ISBN: 978-0997556605
copyright: Robert Lombardo and Kathlyn Glover
2016

Kjg '14

STARTING

NOW

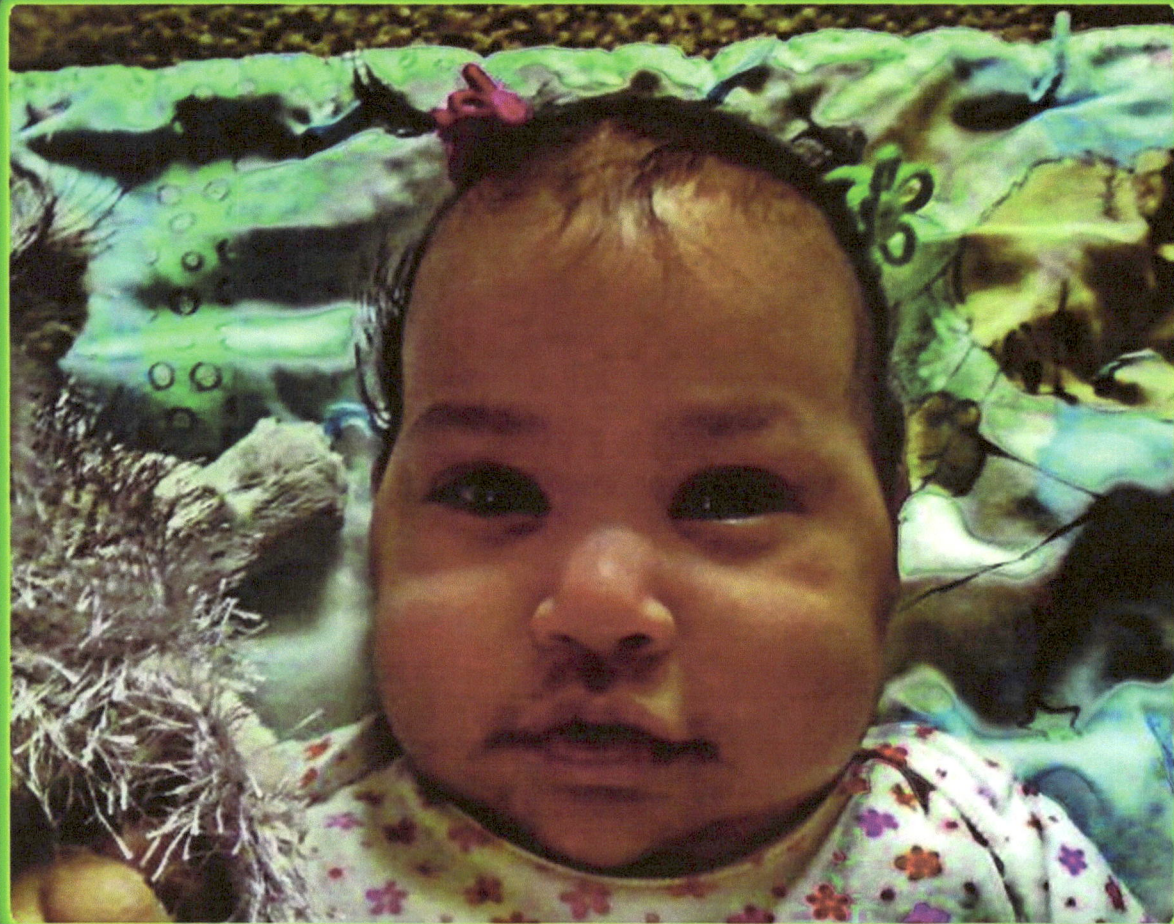

AS EVERY BABY

IS BORN

IN THE WORLD

AND

AS EVERY BABY

RECEIVES THE

GIFTS

OF

LOVE

VALIDATION AND

 POTENTIAL

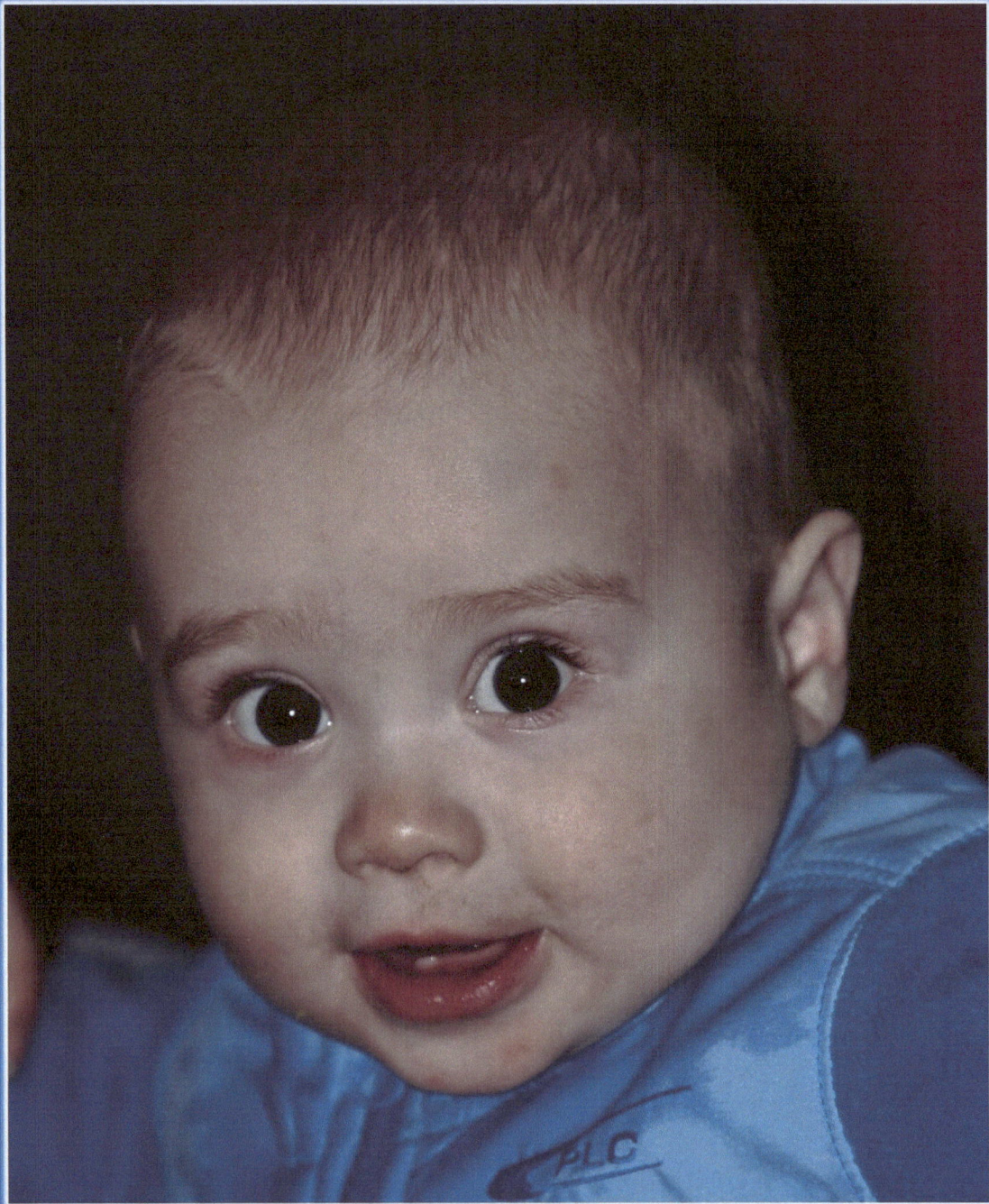

EVERY DAY

THEIR

WHOLE

LIFE

LONG

THE
WORLD
IS
CHANGED

You have just read the vision of Love the Babies as presented in this short book. It is our hope that you will find its simple premise valuable and actionable.

Our web site includes examples of immediate actions you can adopt to spread the message. When humans receive messages of love; validation of worth, contribution and belonging; and support of potential opportunities for creation of a whole happy life, the world is changed. How is it changed? Imagine for yourself. When we imagine, then we begin to notice the support for our imagined ideas.

Why not imagine a world of Love the Babies.

Thank you so much for your positive thoughts for and actions to Love the Babies.

Please turn the page to enjoy more of Kathy's whimsical and uplifting art.

Hjg '14

List of paintings in order

Front cover: Love the Babies
Ecstasy in Blue
City Without Cars
Sitting Room
Flower Grid
Agave
Seven Crows
Many Directions
Fun With Lines and Dots
Campfire
Tipis
Terraces
Kwan Yin
Back cover: Smile

www.ingramcontent.com/pod-product-compliance
Lightning Source LLC
Chambersburg PA
CBHW042121040426
42449CB00003B/139